..Cheeky Messages of Love for You..

..juicylucy..

ℛℛ
RAVETTE PUBLISHING

First published in 2010 by
Ravette Publishing Ltd
P.O. Box 876, Horsham West Sussex RH12 9GH

© 2009 Juicy Lucy Designs
All rights reserved.

www.juicylucydesigns.com

ISBN: 978-1-84161-331-4

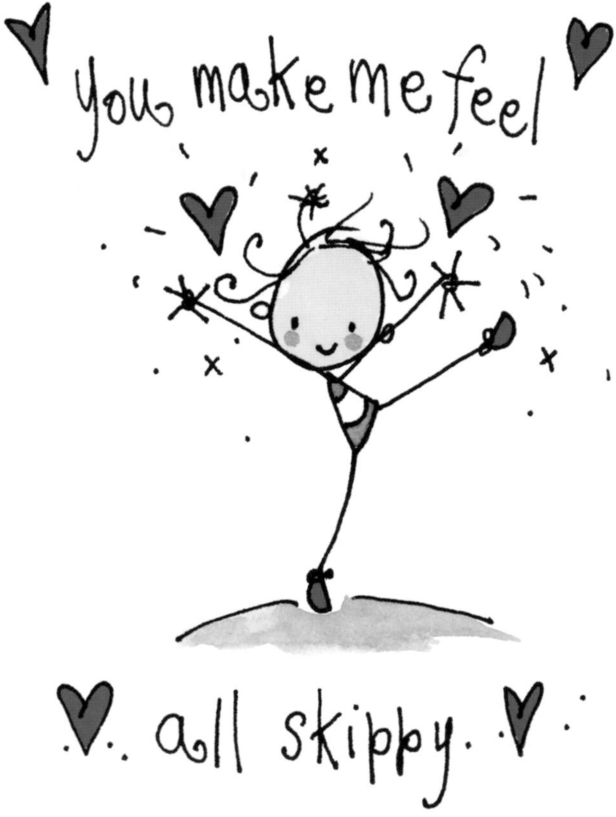
you make me feel
all skippy.

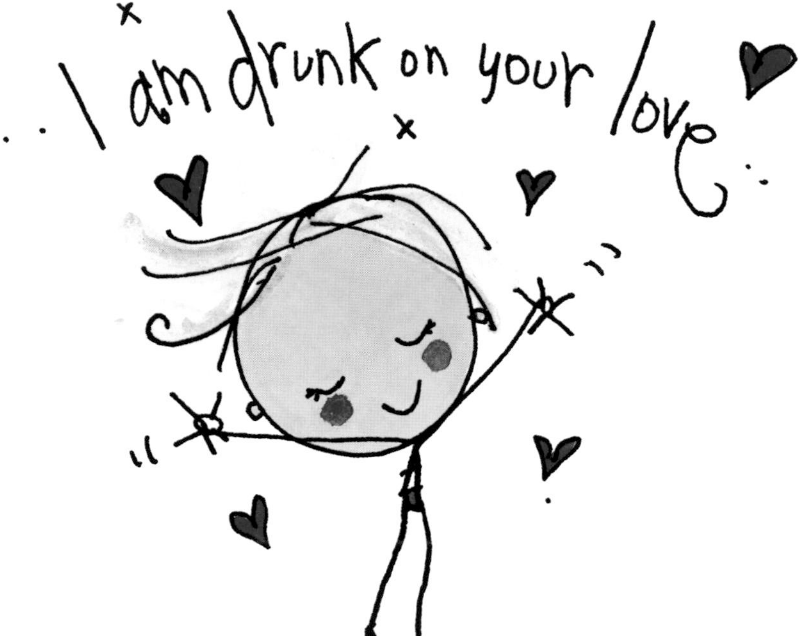
...I am drunk on your love...

let's go wild with gay abandon !

..When you kiss me

it makes my

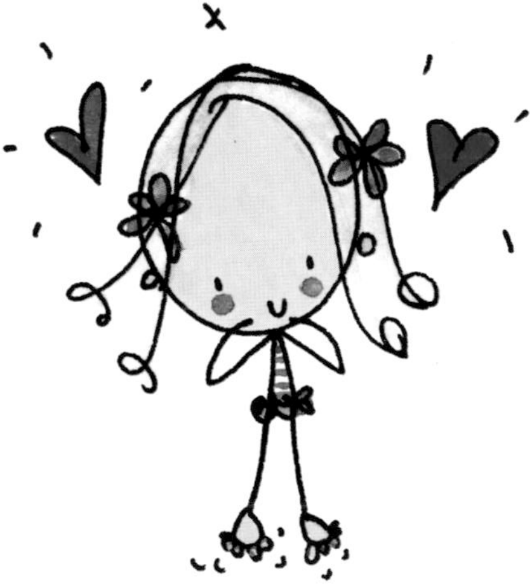

toes wiggle..x

You're not only my best friend

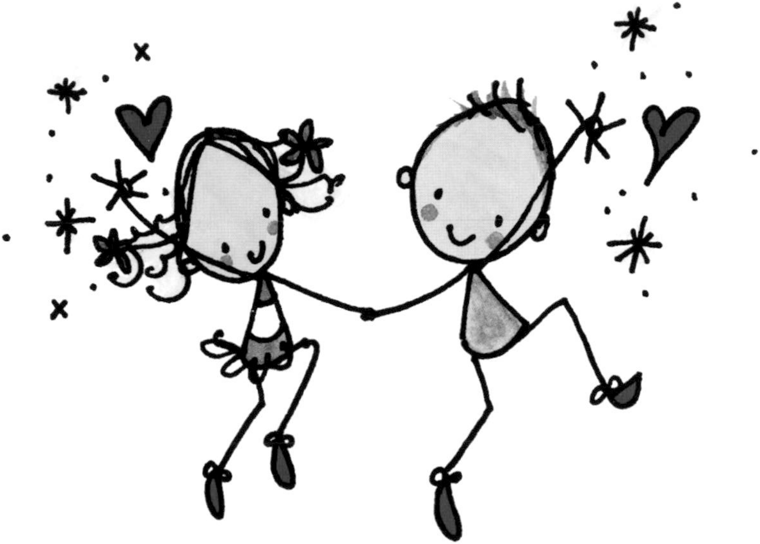

You're also a damn fine shag! x

..I know we sometimes drive eachother..
..crazy..

..but you are the best thing.
in my world..+ I love you..x..

thinking of you makes

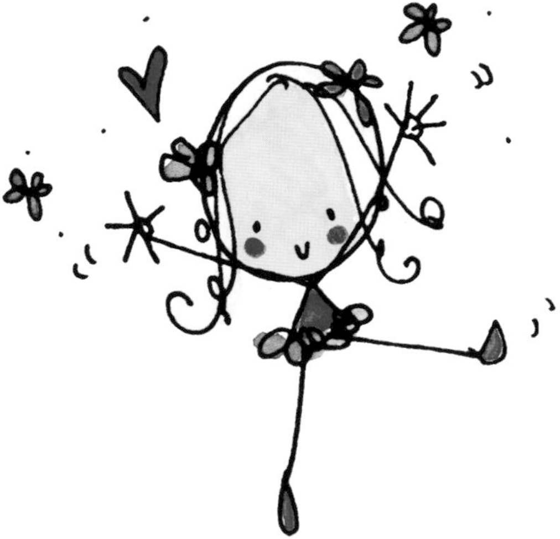

my fanny feel funny!

You make me horny.
x

.. you've got simply gorgeous

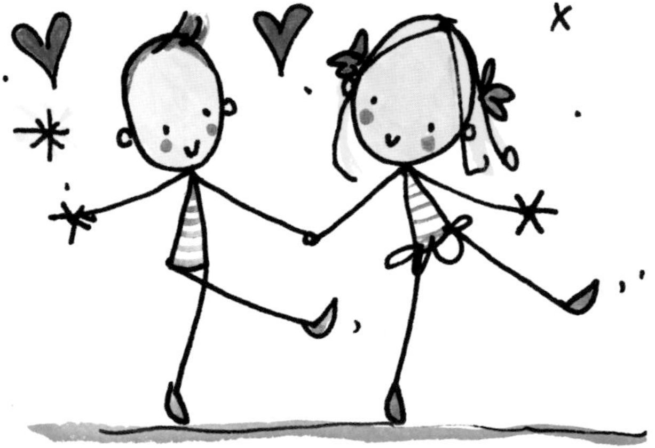

.. goolies .. x

You are the Prince of my Dreams

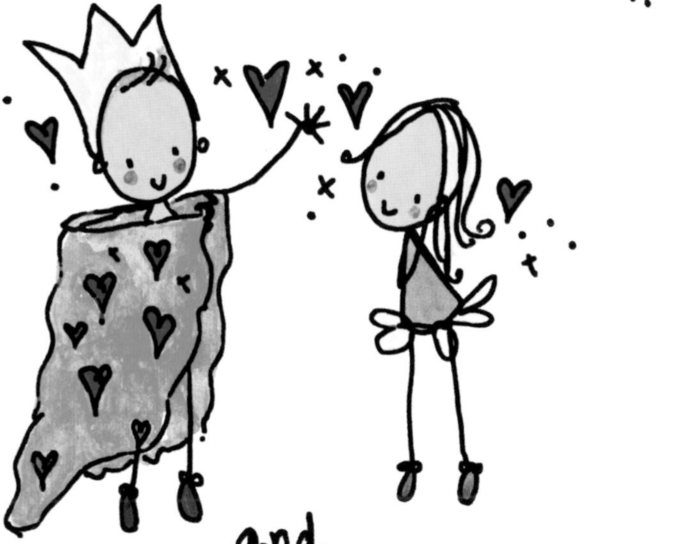

and

the love of my life!

you're my little
chocolate
button
and
I
love
you!
x

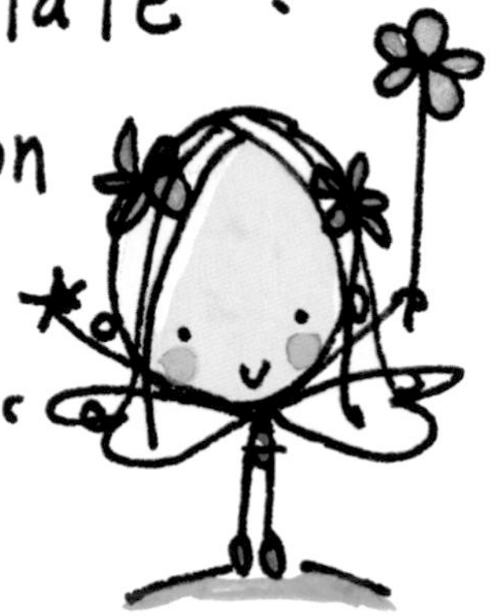

um.. you can do

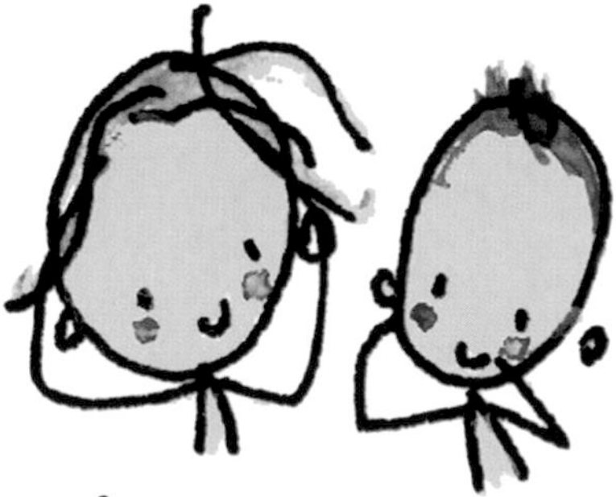

that again

The little fairies think that you are
beautiful and special and kind!
They are thrilled that you have this book,
and want you to know that the lovely
people at Ravette have also published ...

	ISBN	Price
I love you	978-1-84161-298-0	£4.99
I love you mum	978-1-84161-300-0	£4.99
Let's be rudie nudies	978-1-84161-299-7	£4.99
You're a magic mate	978-1-84161-305-5	£4.99

HOW TO ORDER   Please send a cheque/postal order in £ sterling, made
payable to 'Ravette Publishing' for the cover price of the
books and allow the following for post & packaging ...

UK & BFPO   70p for the first book & 40p per book thereafter
Europe & Eire   £1.30 for the first book & 70p per book thereafter
Rest of the world   £2.20 for the first book & £1.10 per book thereafter

RAVETTE PUBLISHING LTD

P.O. Box 876, Horsham, West Sussex RH12 9GH

Tel: 01403 711443   Fax: 01403 711554   Email: ravettepub@aol.com

Prices and availability are subject to change without prior notice.